101

Leadership Reminders

Kimberly Alyn

Copyright © 2004 by Kimberly Alyn

All rights reserved. No part of this book shall be reproduced or transmitted in any form or by any means, electronic, mechanical, magnetic, photographic including photocopying, recording or by any information storage and retrieval system, without prior written permission of the publisher. No patent liability is assumed with respect to the use of the information contained herein. Although every precaution has been taken in the preparation of this book, the publisher and author assume no responsibility for errors or omissions. Neither is any liability assumed for damages resulting from the use of the information contained herein.

ISBN 0-7414-2012-0

Published by:

519 West Lancaster Avenue
Haverford, PA 19041-1413
Info@buybooksontheweb.com
www.buybooksontheweb.com
Toll-free (877) BUY BOOK
Local Phone (610) 520-2500
Fax (610) 519-0261

Printed in the United States of America

Printed on Recycled Paper

Published April 2004

Dedication
ಚಲ

This book is dedicated to Gregory Emil Karels, my Maximus. As I have watched you grow and change through these past few years, I realize now more than ever that you are someone I can truly follow. You inspire me to be a better person and I will always love you.

Acknowledgements

Thank you John Burke for editing another book for me. You do an outstanding job! There are a few close friends in my life who are always there to help push me through when times get tough. In good times and in bad, they stand by my side. Thank you Greg, Joey, and Amanda Karels, Rhonda Catherina, Sam Caniglia, Terri Custer, Sunday Garcia, Samantha Hogle, and the Corwins. You all encourage and inspire me to walk with the Lord, grow in grace, and become the person that God created me to be.

About the Author

Kimberly Alyn is an author and full-time professional speaker and trainer. She is the CEO of Perfect Presentations, a company dedicated to training seminars for a variety of organizations. Kim speaks and trains in corporations, small businesses, and municipalities.

Kim has served as a consultant for a variety of firms and organizations speaking about leadership skills, time and stress management, presentation skills, and various other topics. She also provides keynote speeches on leadership, success strategies, overcoming adversity, juggling a busy life, becoming an effective leader, and coping with the annoying people in life.

A life-long learner, Kim is currently working towards her doctorate in organizational leadership. She is constantly learning and growing as she continues to stretch herself in life.

Kim is the coauthor (with Bob Phillips, Ph.D.) of *Annoying People and Why You're One of Them!* This book addresses social styles, why others annoy us, and why we annoy other people. It's a revolutionary guide to conflict prevention and resolution. It also addresses how to lead and follow the different social styles.

Kim has also authored *Public Speaking is Not for Wimps!* This book serves as a simple guide to giving perfect presentations. Interactive and entertaining presentations are the trademarks of Kim's style. Her many years of experience have enabled her to pass along many valuable insights to other speakers and presenters. She is well-known for taking the driest of topics and turning them into fun and interesting presentations. Kim is also the author of *Soar with Your Savior,* a book that parallels the challenges of flying with Christian living.

Kim has lived on the Central Coast of California since 1979. She has been an active member of her community for many years, serving as a planning commissioner, the president of the Downtown Business Improvement Association, the vice president of Main Street, a Rotary member, and a Chamber of Commerce Member. Kim has also served as a volunteer for a variety of programs and events.

In her spare time, Kim enjoys flying, drawing, and writing. She also likes to spend time with family and friends engaging in outdoor activities. She works hard, plays hard, and loves life!

Introduction
ଔଷଓ

We all need to be reminded now and then of what it takes to be a great leader. The pressures of life often weigh heavily upon us to the point that we lose site of what's truly important. Effective leaders continually remind themselves to focus their energies and prioritize their lives.

This book is intended to assist leaders in staying focused. Pick it up every day and find one reminder to focus on. The concepts and quotes contained within these pages have stood the test of time. All great leaders have embraced these ideas and passed them forward to leaders like you. Engrain them in your heart and pass them on to our next generation of leaders.

1

☙❧
Leadership is the ability to influence others and myself.
☙❧

"Control is not leadership; management is not leadership; leadership is leadership. If you seek to lead, invest at least 50% of your time in leading yourself—your own purpose, ethics, principles, motivation, conduct. Invest at least 20% leading those with authority over you and 15% leading your peers."
— *Dee Hock, Founder and CEO Emeritus, Visa*

2

I need to surround myself with positive and challenging people.

"Keep away from people who try to belittle your ambitions. Small people always do that, but the really great make you feel that you, too, can become great."
—*Mark Twain*

3

❧

To be an effective leader, I have to make sacrifices.

❧

"For anything worth having one must pay the price; and the price is always work, patience, love, self-sacrifice--no paper currency, no promises to pay, but the gold of real service."
—*John Burroughs*

4

Leadership requires vision. I must have a vision for my life, my work, and my purpose.

"A leader has the vision and conviction that a dream can be achieved. He inspires the power and energy to get it done."
—*Ralph Lauren*

"All our dreams can come true, if we have the courage to pursue them."
—*Walt Disney*

5

☙

To be an effective leader, I must take action.

☙

"Vision without action is nothing more than hallucination. Action without vision is nothing more than random activity."
—*Christopher Hegarty*

6

I need to welcome, embrace, and initiate change!

"Your success in life isn't based on your ability to simply change. It is based on your ability to change faster than your competition, customers and business."
—*Mark Sanborn*

7

౪ఐ
To be an effective leader, I must learn to serve others.
౪ఐ

"Servant leadership propels organizational success."
—*Ken Blanchard*

"From now on, any definition of a successful life must include serving others."
—*President George Bush*

101 LEADERSHIP REMINDERS

8

෴

Bad habits will negatively affect my leadership ability.

෴

"The chains of habit are generally too light to be felt until they become too heavy to be broken."
—*Samuel Johnson*

"Bad habits are easier to abandon today than tomorrow."
—*Yiddish Proverb*

9

☙

What I consistently dwell on will determine my mental state and ultimately my course in life.

❧

"Sow a thought, reap an action.
Sow an action, reap a habit.
Sow a habit, reap a character.
Sow a character, reap a destiny."
—*Chinese Proverb*

10

☙❧

If I want excellence in others, I must model it myself.

☙❧

"Whatever is done skillfully appears to be done with ease and art, when it is once matured to habit, vanishes from observation. We are therefore more powerfully excited to emulation by those who have attained the highest degree of excellence, and whom we can therefore with least reason hope to equal."
—*Samuel Johnson*

11

I need to maintain a positive mental outlook if I want to be an effective leader.

"A positive attitude is the one characteristic that all successful people have in common."
—*Anon*

"A happy person is not a person in a certain set of circumstances but rather a person with a certain set of attitudes."
—*Hugh Downs*

12

☙

I need to help facilitate the success of others.

☙

"It is literally true that you can succeed best and quickest by helping others to succeed."
—*Napoleon Hill*

13

⳩

Today is not yesterday, and no matter how many times I have failed before, I can succeed today.

⳩

"Failure will never overtake me if my determination to succeed is strong enough."
—*Og Mandino*

"You always pass failure on your way to success."
—*Mickey Rooney*

101 LEADERSHIP REMINDERS

ಅಸಿಬಿ

I will take responsibility for my choices, my decisions, and my actions.

ಅಸಿಬಿ

"The price of greatness is responsibility."
—*Winston Churchill*

"Success on any major scale requires you to accept responsibility . . . . In the final analysis, the one quality that all successful people have is the ability to take on responsibility."
—*Michael Korda*

15

I will not make excuses.

"The reason people blame things on the previous generation is that there's only one other choice."
—*Doug Larson*

"He that is good for making excuses is seldom good for anything else."
—*Benjamin Franklin*

16

I will learn to listen more and talk less.

"It is the province of knowledge to speak and it is the privilege of wisdom to listen."
—*Oliver Wendall Holmes*

17

I need to seek creative solutions.

"Problems cannot be solved at the same level of awareness that created them."
—*Albert Einstein*

18

☙❧

I will not blame others.

☙❧

"It is ridiculous to lay the blame of our wrong actions upon external causes, rather than on the facility with which we ourselves are caught by such causes."
—*Aristotle*

"Blaming 'society' makes it awfully easy for a person of weak character to shrug off his own responsibility for his actions."
—*Stanley Schmidt*

19

I will not micromanage people.

"Surround yourself with the best people you can find, delegate authority, and don't interfere as long as the policy you've decided upon is being carried out."
—*Ronald Reagan*

20

I will learn to inspire others to greatness.

"Leaders motivate others for a common purpose and inspire others to do something for themselves."
—*Calvin Coolidge*

21

I need to be approachable and accessible.

"Leaders who make it a practice to draw out the thoughts and ideas of their subordinates and who are receptive even to bad news will be properly informed. Communicate downward to subordinates with at least the same care and attention as you communicate upward to superiors."
—L.B. Belker

22

☙❧

I need to remember the names of people I meet.

☙❧

"Own only what you can carry with you; know language, know countries, know people. Let your memory be your travel bag."
—*Alexander Solzhenitsyn*

23

୧୭

I need to greet people with enthusiasm.

୧୭

"Enthusiasm is the yeast that makes your hopes shine to the stars. Enthusiasm is the sparkle in your eyes, the swing in your gait. The grip of your hand, the irresistible surge of will and energy to execute your ideas."
—*Henry Ford*

24

ೞ

To be an effective leader, I must follow through on my commitments.

ೞ

"People do not follow uncommitted leaders. Commitment can be displayed in a full range of matters to include the work hours you choose to maintain, how you work to improve your abilities, or what you do for your fellow workers at personal sacrifice."
— *Stephen Gregg, Chairman and CEO of Ethix Corp*

25

ଔଷୠ

I need to be on time and prepared.

ଔଷୠ

"Success depends upon previous preparation, and without such preparation there is sure to be failure."
—*Confucius*

"If I had six hours to chop down a tree, I'd spend the first hour sharpening the ax."
—*Abraham Lincoln*

26

ଓଷ୍ଠ

I must learn to balance confidence with humility.

ଓଷ୍ଠ

"Being in power is a lot like being a lady. If you have to tell people you are then you aren't."
—*Margaret Thatcher*

27

ಚ೫

I need to value the opinions of others.

ಚ೫

"The moment we begin to fear the opinions of others and hesitate to tell the truth that is in us, and from motives of policy are silent when we should speak, the divine floods of light and life no longer flow into our souls."
—*Elizabeth Cady Stanton*

28

To be an effective leader, I must prioritize.

"Not everything that can be counted counts,
and not everything that counts can be counted."
—*Albert Einstein*

29

I have to be willing to take risks.

"Avoiding danger is no safer in the long run than outright exposure. Life is either a daring adventure, or nothing."
—*Helen Keller*

30

To be an effective leader, I have to remain teachable.

"As long as you're green, you're growing. As soon as you're ripe, you start to rot."
—*Ray Kroc*

"Leadership and learning are indispensable to each other."
—*John F. Kennedy*

31

ଓଥବ

I need to have a sense of humor about life and lighten up!

ଓଥବ

"I like nonsense; it wakes up the brain cells. Fantasy is a necessary ingredient in living; it's a way of looking at life through the wrong end of a telescope. Which is what I do, and that enables you to laugh at life's realities."
—*Dr. Seuss*

32

⊰❦⊱

When problems arise I need to ask myself, "What can I learn from this?"

⊰❦⊱

"The measure of success is not whether you have a tough problem to deal with, but whether it is the same problem you had last year."
—*John Foster Dulles*

33

To be an effective leader I have to take care of myself by exercising and eating healthy.

"He who has health has hope; and he who has hope has everything."
—*Arabian Proverb*

34

☙

I will spend the majority of my time focusing on solutions, not problems.

☙

"The majority see the obstacles; the few see the objectives; history records the successes of the latter, while oblivion is the reward of the former."
— *Alfred Armand Montapert*

35

ෲ
I need to remain hopeful in the face of adversity.
ෲ

"All the adversity I've had in my life, all my troubles and obstacles, have strengthened me... You may not realize it when it happens, but a kick in the teeth may be the best thing in the world for you."
—*Walt Disney*

36

ଓଷ୍ଟ

I will avoid people who wallow in negativity.

ଓଷ୍ଟ

"Get rid of the negative people in your life—surround yourself with positive people who believe in you and inspire you."
—*Unknown*

37

☙❧

The quality of my life is directly related to the quality of my choices.

☙❧

"The course of our lives is not determined by great, awesome decisions. Our direction is set by the little day-to-day choices which chart the track on which we run."
—*Gordon B. Hinckley*

38

Mediocrity is not an option!

"Great spirits have always found violent opposition from mediocre minds. The latter cannot understand it when a man does not thoughtlessly submit to hereditary prejudices but honestly and courageously uses his intelligence and fulfills the duty to express the results of his thoughts in clear form."
—*Albert Einstein*

39

I am only a true leader when people follow me because they want to, not because they have to.

"He who thinks he leads but has no followers is only taking a walk."
—*Leadership Proverb*

40

☙❧

My age does not determine my youth; my attitude does!

☙❧

"Human beings, by changing the inner attitudes of their minds, can change the outer aspects of their lives."
—*William James*

41

Increasing my knowledge in my field will increase my effectiveness.

"Knowledge is, indeed, that which, next to virtue, truly and essentially raises one man above another."
—*Joseph Addison*

"Education is learning what you didn't even know you didn't know."
—*Daniel J. Boorstin*

42

ಉತ್ತರ

Everything I do today will either move me towards my goals or away from them.

ಉತ್ತರ

"The most important key to achieving great success is to decide upon your goal and launch, get started, take action, move."
—*Brian Tracy*

43

☙❧

To be an effective leader, I must be proactive, not reactionary.

☙❧

"It has been my observation that most people get ahead during the time that others waste time."
—*Henry Ford*

44

I need to give to others without expecting anything in return.

"You must give some time to your fellow men. Even if it's a little thing, do something for others - something for which you get no pay but the privilege of doing it."
—*Albert Schweitzer*

45

As an effective leader, I need to avoid unproductive arguments.

"In most instances, all an argument proves is that two people are present."
—*Tony Petito*

46

Ethical shortcuts are not an option.

"That you may retain your self-respect, it is better to displease the people by doing what you know is right, than to temporarily please them by doing what you know is wrong."
—*William J. H. Boetcker*

47

To be an effective leader, I need to express sincere appreciation.

"Appreciation is a wonderful thing. It makes what is excellent in others belong to us as well."
—*Voltaire*

48

I will speak my mind with respect.

"Being brilliant is no great feat if you respect nothing."
—*Johann Wolfgang von Goethe*

49

I will not waste time dwelling on the past.

"The farther behind I leave the past, the closer I am to forging my own character."
—*Isabelle Eberhardt*

101 LEADERSHIP REMINDERS

50

ଔଔ

I need to set my goals high.

ଔଔ

"It's better to shoot for the moon and hit an eagle than to shoot for an eagle and hit a rock."
—*Unknown*

51

Giving up is not an option.

"People of mediocre ability sometimes achieve outstanding success because they don't know when to quit. Most men succeed because they are determined to."
—*George Herbert Allen*

52

As an effective leader, I have to be aware of how my actions affect others.

"Man must cease attributing his problems to his environment, and learn again to exercise his will – his personal responsibility."
—*Albert Schweitzer*

53

I will leave my baggage at the door before I come to work.

"Four fifths of all our troubles in this life would disappear, if we would only sit down and keep still."
—*Calvin Coolidge*

54

☙❧

I cannot manage people; I must lead them by positive influence.

☙❧

"Management is nothing more than motivating other people."
—*Lee Iacocca*

55

If I want respect, I need to give it.

"Respect is love in plain clothes."
— *Frankie Byrne*

56

To be an effective leader, I must have vision.

"The very essence of leadership is that you have a vision. It's got to be a vision you articulate clearly and forcefully on every occasion. You can't blow an uncertain trumpet."
— *Theodore Hesburgh*

57

I will believe in the perceived impossible.

"Big thinking precedes great achievement."
—*Wilferd Peterson*

"The future belongs to those who see possibilities before they become obvious."
—*John Scully*

58

I need to have a quality mentor in my life.

"If the blind lead the blind, both shall fall in the ditch."
—*Jesus Christ*

59

To accomplish my goals, I have to remain focused.

"Keep focused on the substantive issues. To make a decision means having to go through one door and closing all others."
— *Abraham Zaleznik*

60

I will have passion and purpose for my work and my life.

"One person with passion is better than forty people merely interested."
— *E. M. Forster*

"Nobody can be successful unless he loves his work."
— *David Sarnoff, CEO of RCA*

61

༺༻

Character DOES matter.

༺༻

"The respect that leadership must have requires that one's ethics be without question. A leader not only stays above the line between right and wrong, he stays well clear of the gray areas."
— *G. Alan Bernard, President, Mid Park, Inc.*

62

I will strive for the highest quality possible in all that I do.

"The society which scorns excellence in plumbing because plumbing is a humble activity and tolerates shoddiness in philosophy because it is an exalted activity will have neither good plumbing nor good philosophy. Neither its pipes nor its theories will hold water."
— *John Gardner*

63

ॐ

The power of my smile can make someone's day.

ॐ

"Every time you smile at someone, it is an action of love, a gift to that person, a beautiful thing."
—*Mother Teresa*

64

I must face my fears.

"You gain strength, courage, and confidence by every experience in which you really stop to look fear in the face."
— *Eleanor Roosevelt*

"Courage is doing what you're afraid to do. There can be no courage unless you're scared."
— *Eddie Rickenbacker*

65

ଓଽୠ

To be an effective leader, I can not procrastinate.

ଓଽୠ

"The leading rule for the lawyer, as for the man of every other calling, is diligence. Leave nothing for tomorrow which can be done today."
— *Abraham Lincoln*

66

I am not an island unto myself; I need others to be successful.

"Teamwork is the ability to work together toward a common vision. The ability to direct individual accomplishments toward organizational objectives. It is the fuel that allows common people to attain uncommon results."
—*Andrew Carnegie*

67

To be an effective leader, I must be consistent.

"Fall seven times, stand up eight."
—*Japanese Proverb*

68

I need to be a positive role model.

"You cannot be a leader, and ask other people to follow you, unless you know how to follow too."
—*Sam Rayburn*

69

☙

I will persevere until I succeed.

☙

"It is inevitable that some defeat will enter even the most victorious life. The human spirit is never finished when it is defeated... it is finished when it surrenders."
—*Ben Stein*

70

The circumstances in my life do not define me.

> "Only 10% of life is what happens to you. 90% is how you choose to react to it."
> —*Charles Swindoll*

71

To be an effective leader, I need to forgive.

"To err is human, to forgive, divine."
—*Alexander Pope*

"He that cannot forgive others breaks the bridge over which he must pass himself; for every man has need to be forgiven."
—*Lord Herbert*

72

I will involve stakeholders in the decision-making process.

"Alone we can do so little; together we can do so much."
—*Helen Keller*

73

I will always strive to improve.

"There's only one corner of the universe you can be certain of improving, and that's your own self."
—*Aldous Huxley*

"If you wish to achieve worthwhile things in your personal and career life, you must become a worthwhile person in your own self-development."
—*Brian Tracy*

74

I will face each task with determination.

"Nothing in the world can take the place of persistence. Talent will not; nothing is more common than unsuccessful men with talent. Genius will not; unrewarded genius is almost a proverb. Education will not; the world is full of educated derelicts. Persistence and determination alone are omnipotent."
—*Calvin Collidge*

75

Arrogance will get me nowhere as a leader; humility will serve me well.

"Many people believe that humility is the opposite of pride, when, in fact, it is a point of equilibrium. The opposite of pride is actually a lack of self esteem. A humble person is totally different from a person who cannot recognize and appreciate himself as part of this worlds marvels."
—*Rabino Nilton Bonder*

76

To be an effective leader, I must constantly improve my communication skills.

"Precision of communication is important, more important than ever, in our era of hair trigger balances, when a false or misunderstood word may create as much disaster as a sudden thoughtless act."
—*James Thurber*

77

I will live by the positive values that I proclaim.

"It is easier to fight for one's principles than to live up to them."
—*Alfred Adler*

78

I will foster an atmosphere of trust as I hold things in confidence.

"Make it your guiding principle to do your best for others and to be trustworthy in what you say."
—*Confucius*

78

I will look at many alternatives to solving problems.

"Never accept the proposition that just because a solution satisfies a problem, that it must be the only solution."
—Raymond E. Feist

79

I will not lead people by intimidation.

"A boss creates fear, a leader confidence. A boss fixes blame, a leader corrects mistakes. A boss knows all, a leader asks questions. A boss makes work drudgery, a leader makes it interesting. A boss is interested in himself or herself, a leader is interested in the group."
—*Russel H. Ewing*

80

As an effective leader, I will stand up for what I believe in.

"Common experience shows how much rarer is moral courage than physical bravery. A thousand men will march to the mouth of the cannon where one man will dare espouse an unpopular cause."
—*Clarence Darrow*

81

☙

I will strive to be more generous each day.

☙

"No person was ever honored for what he received. Honor has been the reward for what he gave."
—*Calvin Coolidge*

82

Temporary setbacks will not discourage me from trying again.

"Develop success from failures. Discouragement and failure are two of the surest stepping stones to success."
— *Dale Carnegie*

83

I can always learn something from everyone.

"Even when walking in the company of two other men, I am bound to be able to learn from them. The good points of the one I copy; the bad points of the other I correct in myself."
—*Confucius*

84

To be an effective leader, I must be fair at all times.

"Ethics is not about the way things are, it is about the way things ought to be."
—*Michael Josephson*

"Thou shouldst not decide until thou hast heard what both have to say."
—*Aristophanes*

85

ೞ೦

I will not be afraid to try new things.

ೞ೦

"I would rather regret the things I have done than the things I have not."
—*Lucille Ball*

86

ೞ

I will model the work ethic I desire in others.

ೞ

"Men acquire a particular quality by constantly acting in a particular way."
—*Aristotle*

87

I will coach and support those around me.

"A leader is best when people barely know he exists, not so good when people obey and acclaim him, worst when they despise him. But of a good leader, who talks little, when his work is done, his aim fulfilled, they will say, 'We did this ourselves.'"
— *Lao-Tse*

88

To be an effective leader, I must be decisive.

"If I had to sum up in a word what makes a good manager, I'd say decisiveness. You can use the fanciest computers to gather the numbers, but in the end you have to set a timetable and act."
— *Lee J. Iacocca*

89

I will actively listen to others.

"The best way to persuade people is with your ears—
by listening to them."
— *Dean Rusk*

90

○₃₈○

When I am wrong, I will admit I am wrong.

○₃₈○

"Life is a long lesson in humility."
— *James M. Barrie*

91

To be an effective leader, I need to learn to say "I'm sorry."

"Pride is concerned with *who* is right.
Humility is concerned with *what* is right."
— *Ezra Taft Benson*

92

☙❧

I must exercise patience in all that I do.

☙❧

"Learn the art of patience. Apply discipline to your thoughts when they become anxious over the outcome of a goal. Impatience breeds anxiety, fear, discouragement and failure. Patience creates confidence, decisiveness, and a rational outlook, which eventually leads to success."
—*Brian Adams*

93

I will continually motivate those around me.

"In motivating people, you've got to engage their minds and their hearts. It is good business to have an employee feel part of the entire effort . . . I motivate people, I hope, by example—and perhaps by excitement, by having provocative ideas to make others feel involved."
— *Rupert Murdoch*

94

I will constantly strive to build better relationships.

"I am convinced that nothing we do is more important than hiring and developing people. At the end of the day you bet on people, not on strategies."
— *Larry Bossidy, CEO, Allied Signal*

95

I will make myself accountable to others.

"It is easy to dodge our responsibilities, but we cannot dodge the consequences of dodging our responsibilities."
—*Sir Josiah Stamp*

96

I will fix myself before I attempt to fix others.

"You can never conquer the mountain.
You can only conquer yourself."
— *Jim Whittaker*

97

To be an effective leader, I need to serve others.

"The true leader serves. Serves people. Serves their best interests, and in doing so will not always be popular, may not always impress. But because true leaders are motivated more by loving concern than a desire for personal glory, they are willing to pay the price."
— *Eugene B. Habecker*

98

I need to take a "bottom-up" approach to leadership.

"If you don't understand that you work for your mislabeled 'subordinates,' then you know nothing of leadership. You know only tyranny."
— *Dee Hock, Founder and CEO Emeritus*
VISA International

99

I will allow my followers to discover their own processes.

"The best executive is one who has sense enough to pick good people to do what he wants done, and self-restraint enough to keep from meddling with them while they do it."
— *Theodore Roosevelt*

100

People are more important than money.

"People are more important than money, power, time and stuff."
— *Rev. Alan W. Hinden*

101

I need to keep reminding myself that I am a work in progress.

"Become addicted to constant and never ending self improvement."
—*Anthony J. D'Angelo*

How to Order Books

Log on to any of these sites:
Amazon.com
BarnesAndNoble.com
PerfectPresentations.net

**OR CALL:
1-800-821-8116**

To order a signed copy, send an e-mail to:
Kim@PerfectPresentations.net

For more information about Kim Alyn, her speaking services, and training workshops, log on to:
PerfectPresentations.net

To order other books written by Kim Alyn, log on to:
PerfectPresentations.net

How to Schedule Kimberly Alyn for a Speaking Engagement

Call:
1-800-821-8116

or
Log on to:
PerfectPresentations.net

*I love the grasshopper.
Grasshoppers can leap 20 times the length of their own
bodies as they soar through the air. I want to learn to soar
like that—far beyond the length of my perceived limitations!*

Printed in the United States
46929LVS00002B/10